Listen up!

By Yvonne Prentice

Copyright

Acknowledgements

I am so amazed at how God has orchestrated my life in drawing me into friendship with Him. It is because of the Father's love for me and, I might add, for you also dear reader that Jesus came and gave His all to bring us into His family. Thank God for that totally selfless act that has taken away the sin barrier and given us the Divine gift of God the Spirit. Holy Spirit is the inspirer of this book and I must acknowledge that without the grace of Holy Spirit this book would not be possible. God's voice has become my daily bread. I am so thankful.

There are several people who have helped in the making of this book. Many thanks to:

Bob Prentice: My amazing husband who always cheers me on; just the best guy on the planet. Love you Bob.

Karin Trory: The proofreading job is always done so willingly and with such enthusiasm. You're awesome.

Rev. Virginia Tilstra: You are an inspiration, a woman who lives by listening to God and a great ministry partner.

Irene & Randy Rennick: So good to be on team Jesus with you both. You live the reality of Christ in us. So cool!

Rev. Glenda Bromell: Thank you for your expert help in the editing of this book.

Contents

Introduction

The adventure of learning to listen and hear God is different for each of us. Just as we have different stories about how we are born in the natural we all have a different journey to God. We are born for a reason. God has a great purpose for us here on earth, but even more than that God, wants us to enjoy friendship with Him.

It is amazing to think our friendship is what God had in mind when He created the earth and everything on it! A big clue to the reason and purpose for our creation is revealed in the way God chose to be near the first people[1]. We see that before He created Eve, God was with Adam, bringing him the animals to see what Adam would name them. He was with Adam in his work.

God also enjoyed the cool of each day with the family He created (Eve being created from Adam), walking together with Adam and Eve in the Garden of Eden[2]. Their communication was unhindered. God's presence was most keenly noticeable to the first people as they had this pleasant time, enjoying Him. Man finds satisfaction and meaning in work but God's pleasure is to be with us. His true joy is in sharing His thoughts, companionship, and in communicating His love to us.

God's desire to create living beings capable of receiving His love, with the capacity to enjoy His company, was fulfilled back then in the garden of Eden and with His friends today. God's purpose for creating us was not that we work for Him, but that we will enjoy being with Him. He wants us to receive His love and love Him in return. I believe God desires that we have an even closer relationship with Him than Adam and Eve did. He desires us to live in constant connection with Him.

What was lost due to disobedience at the tree of the knowledge of good and evil has been reinstated by Jesus at the 'tree' of the cross. His great sacrifice, death, burial, resurrection, and ascension, made possible the reinstatement

---

1   Genesis 2:19
2   Genesis 3:8

of the communion mankind once experienced in the garden. He has made this life of friendship possible if we will choose to receive His offer of forgiveness and cleansing. The choice to be near Him is ours but we must come on His terms. This means receiving forgiveness and reinstatement as God's children through the blood payment of Jesus Christ. We do not have to pay the price, but we do have to turn back to Him in connection and communication with Him.

It is God's design that we take hold of our purpose and turn our attention toward Him. As I mentioned, I feel God's desire for unhindered communion (common union)[3] goes further than restoring us to the level of friendship Adam and Eve had. God's passion is that we live united with Him through the Holy Spirit every moment of the day, not just for short little devotional moments. He wants to be invited into the garden of our spirit, to restore our soul as well as giving life and light to our understanding. That is why Jesus Christ gave up His life. His act of sacrifice paid not only for original sin (the disobedience of Adam and Eve) and personal sin (our own acts of disobedience), but dealt a death blow to the sin nature which has kept each of us from friendship with God. This garden of friendship (or Eden) is now open to us 24/7 as a continuous spirit- to-Spirit connection with God.

You will find in this little book some keys for unlocking the door to knowing God's voice. As you read and work through the listening prayer exercises I trust you will find the pleasure of knowing the One who made you. God has a beautiful plan for your life and I pray you will be led into it by taking His lead and following the path Jesus has marked out for you.

---

3   Definition of common: meaning together or belonging to all. Definition of union: oneness, the act of joining two and forming a compound body.

Hearing With More Than Ears
The Ways God Speaks

All of us learn to communicate from our earliest days. We use spoken language which we learn from our parents or caregivers. Children also learn to recognize what people are saying by the body language people use. We learn from a young age that body language shows more meaning than the spoken words alone. In fact, you can often tell what someone is really saying by looking at how they are positioned. If a person is sitting with arms and legs folded and leaning back they are probably not very open to the conversation around them. On the other hand, if they are leaning forward looking intently at the person speaking we can easily tell they are interested and listening carefully. We can often tell when a friend is upset, depressed, angry, or happy by their body language.

In a similar way, all of us have at least one way or language through which we can hear God. This chapter is a short review of the ways God speaks to us. Most Christians recognize the Bible as their main way to hear God, but we also have other languages or ways we hear God. We can, if we choose, learn to hear God in different ways just as we can learn other spoken languages. Even when God is not using words to talk we can learn to interpret what He wants us to know, a bit like reading the body language of someone.

We communicate in many ways when we are at a distance from others, whether by email, Facebook, Twitter, greeting cards, or sending gifts. We can be quite creative in communicating, so since God is the Creator, He is amazing at communication. God is continuously speaking messages of love, encouragement, comfort, wisdom, correction, direction, and more. He wants to help and guide us so that we receive all the benefit of His great wisdom and care. He does not want us to be directionless and lost. God really wants to be our life long – even eternal friend. He doesn't want us to miss anything He has planned for us.

Often God speaks through the mysteries or puzzles of life's circumstances, nature, our senses, our emotions, dreams, music, and media. These messages are often not clear to us at first. They are starting points of the conversation He wants to have with us, like an opening or one-liner of a conversation. When you see a strange natural occurrence, notice a road sign or newspaper headline, when you notice something unusual or outstanding around you, Holy Spirit is actually saying…"Will you look at that…That's something I want you to take note of!"

Everyday occurrences can be opportunities for God to speak on a topic we are wondering about. God loves us. He loves to chat with us, so let's take the hint and chat life over with Him.

As you read this chapter, I encourage you to find your first language in God. Ask Him to expand your ways of hearing Him. He loves to speak to you and knows everything about every subject...After all, He is God!

Hearing God through the Bible

The Bible is the usual way most Christians hear from God. It is not only a great book to read as a historical account but also shows us the way God acted toward people and how people learned about Him - sometimes through disobeying and other times through following Him.

The Bible is more than a book though it has a supernatural aspect to it. The Bible can come alive and speak to your situation every day if you read it looking for God's answers. If we ask the Holy Spirit to show us how the reading fits into our lives He will. He makes the written words become alive and helpful for the things that are happening around us today. Through meditative reading (slow, thoughtful, and repetitive), we often sense God's voice pointing to particular words, verses, and passages of Scripture which relate to our need. It can be almost like the words are highlighted to us by the Holy Spirit and we 'get' what God wants to tell us.

The Bible our testing tool: We know from 2 Timothy 3:16 that all Scripture is God-breathed and is useful for teaching, correcting and training in righteousness.

The Bible is the Logos or written word, and a passage highlighted by Holy Spirit is the Rhema or personal word to us[4]. Not only is the Bible our primary way of being guided by God, it is the best tool for testing all the other ways we feel we are hearing from Him. We can test the spirit of the messages we think are from God and tell or discern whether they are God thoughts, our own thoughts, or evil/ negative thoughts.

The Bible reveals the nature and character of God. We can tell if the message we are receiving lines up with who God is. For example, His character or nature is loving, pure,

---

4   A further distinction between the two Greek terms *Rhema* and *Logos* can help us grasp two aspects of God's "Word". *Rhema*, at times called "Spoken Word", refers to the revelation received by us when Holy Spirit speaks to our hearts, as referred to in John 14:17, 26. *Logos* refers to the Word of God, the person of Christ, the Bible from Genesis to Revelation.

kind, just, and so on. His written word helps us judge every other way God speaks. However the message comes, through words, pictures, feelings or leadings we think are from God, they must be in agreement with the principles of the Bible. For more about this see the chapter called Checking It Out.

Our Circumstances

God will often get our attention through unusual or troubling circumstances in order to cause us to stop and ask for direction. Sometimes we become too distracted to hear Him, so God will allow change to occur that will slow us down long enough to ask Him for help and wait for His answer.

Negative things that disappoint us can cause us to come to Him for guidance. Job loss, sickness, or relational problems may draw us to Him for wisdom and help. Blessings also carry the potential for us to come to God; for example, a new job, being chosen for a special position, a financial windfall, and other positive changes could remind us of our need for wisdom and cause us to seek God for it. He can use a shift in our circumstances to refocus our lives and to move us into our destiny.

Natural Surroundings

God will speak to us through the world around us and the people we interact with every day, especially if we have asked Him a question or are asking for wisdom and direction. Our part in hearing Him is to be open and aware that the One who created us wants to guide and answer our questions. Often the voice of God comes as we go about life, doing everyday activities. Holy Spirit is the one who alerts us to notice when God is using our circumstances, natural surroundings, or the words of other people.

God has spoken to me through weather changes, earthquakes, trees, flowers, insects, animal and human behaviour, along with signs on buildings and vehicles. He is so very creative in the way He communicates!

I have been given wisdom through animals and birds

when Holy Spirit has quickened me to notice a different behaviour or something unusual. For example, a pair of raccoons once came to a very spindly tree in my yard in the country and perched on a branch in broad daylight. There was very little foliage to hide them and when our family took notice, the animals just kept very still and 'played possum' as we say in Australia, meaning they pretended to be asleep or dead.

This behaviour was so unusual I felt God was speaking through it. As I later prayed and thought about the raccoon couple's odd behaviour I realized God was giving me insight into the character of a young couple our family had been helping.

Raccoons are masked and these ones were trying to deceive us into thinking they were just sleeping, not up to anything like getting into the garbage and making a mess! The young couple too were pretending and had the potential of causing a big mess for us if we let them. We were able to help them from a distance and avoid the mess they could have created for us because of their love of 'garbage' which was sin in their case.

An amazing incident my husband Bob witnessed serves as another example of God speaking through what is 'un-naturally' natural. He was taking a lunch break in the parking lot of the company he worked for at the time when he saw something fall from the sky and hit a shiny new blue truck of a co-worker. The co-worker had just lovingly polished and parked his new truck away from the other vehicles in order to keep it safe from any accidents or dust. The object fell from seemingly nowhere and hit the truck with such force it bent the antenna backward then slid across the parking lot coming to a stop some distance away. Other men on their break heard the impact but only Bob saw the object which turned out to be a fish, specifically a carp which is a very large freshwater fish. Bob took pictures of the gasping fish and called the shocked owner of the truck to see the cause of the bent antenna and bloodied mess on the hood of his beloved truck.

At the time of the impact, Bob had been wondering what he was doing working in this particular place. God's message to him was provision and evangelism, both of which are linked for Bob who loves to evangelize in his workplace. God was confirming and encouraging Bob; also, perhaps the man who owned the truck needed to straighten his antenna and listen up because God was trying to get his attention too!

People

Most of us expect to hear God through a pastor or spiritual leader, but interestingly, God can and regularly does speak through everyday people we meet. The Bible says, "God is not a respecter of persons", meaning no matter who we are or what status people place on us, God sees all people of equal value. This is very much the case when He is communicating with us. God will speak through a homeless person or millionaire with equal significance to our life. The interpreter is Holy Spirit who helps us to realize it was from God.

I have noticed God speaking to me through ministers, prophets, cashiers, people on radio, TV, YouTube and even little children. All were God's voice to me, even though many of these people did not know they were speaking for God. Some of them would have been shocked at the thought! Nonetheless, God used what they said to speak me.

Dreams

God has spoken through dreams and visions all through the Old and New Testament. In fact, one-third of the Bible is talking about them. Dreams are like a detective story; a number of clues are given in a dream which need to be pieced together to reveal the message. The interpretation may be quite different than what would have appeared to be communicated on the surface, as dreams are often symbolic. They can come from God, your own mind or emotion, or can even be from the enemy. We need to learn to discern where they are coming from. It is important to pray before you go to sleep, asking God to give you only His dreams and to protect your mind (if not all of you) as you sleep.

Many people have blockages to their dream life because of unbelief, fear of nightmares, or because they have spoken curses over their ability to dream ("I don't dream", "I never remember my dreams", etc.). If this is the case, repentance and cleansing of the imagination will restore your ability to receive dreams. In the case of nightmares, it could be that there is an opening for the enemy due to polluting of the imagination (for example, watching horror movies, explicit and violent visual material, etc.). This too can be repented of, and our dream life rededicated.

Dreams need interpretation. You will understand why as you read about the dream below:

PATNA, INDIA: A 22-year-old man jumped into the tiger's cage at Sanjay Gandhi Botanical Garden in Patna on Saturday to release the big cat from its enclosure. Mohammad Imran Khan is a resident of the village Piroo in Aurangabad district. The first year BA student said that he has been in Patna for the past few days and had a dream last night that he had to set the tiger free and that it wouldn't kill him. Although he was badly mauled he was able to speak from the hospital, "See, it didn't kill me", he said[5].

As we can see from this weird story, we need to be careful to interpret our dreams using wisdom and guidance from the Holy Spirit because they usually symbolize things and are not meant to be taken literally. Many times God will give the interpretation as we journal[6]. Dreams are often larger-than-life kind of videos which exaggerate circumstances to get our attention. Sometimes people are troubled by dreams when they are really just symbolic for what is happening at home, work, or school. Often people worry about something terrible in a dream. For example, when someone dies, the death may actually be about the end of a relationship or the end of a time period the person represents to us.

5   TNN (August 11, 2013) "Man Jumps into Tiger Cage to Set it Free", the Times of India – story: http://articles.timesofindia.indiatimes.com/2013-08-11/patna/41293968_1_patna-zoo-tiger-cage-big-cat
6   See Chapter 3 on journaling the words of God

Knowledge of Bible, cultural and personal symbolism is very helpful in interpreting. However, even more important is that we develop friendship with God. He will give us the ability to interpret our dreams so that they become helpful in understanding God's direction and wisdom for our lives.

Emotion

God can use our emotions to speak to us about our own needs, the needs of others, and the spiritual atmosphere of our surroundings. Emotions can also show how He feels about a situation or person. Holy Spirit has often given me the emotions of a person I am praying for so I can pray with compassion. I have also felt the emotion-charged atmosphere when I have come into a place where prayer is needed. For example, when I am prayer-walking a neighbourhood, I can tangibly feel the change in atmosphere. Once, when I had crossed a street and walked into a certain neighbourhood, I felt the hopelessness, depression, and anger of the residents, so I prayed for God's help and provision as well as His love, peace, and joy to prevail there.

We can often feel God's heart or emotions for the people we are praying for. This emotional burden-bearing for God is a wonderful gift given to help us pray. As we hear God through emotions we need to use discernment by asking God where this emotion is coming from. He will give us understanding so we can pray or help others. Once we have prayed, we need to give the emotion and responsibility back to God – those things are not ours to keep carrying. It is awesome when God shares His heart with us so we can join in the work He wants to do.

Inner Knowing

Many people hear God inwardly Spirit-to-spirit. They just know what God is saying. Spirit-to-spirit is how most revelation comes to us. The Holy Spirit communicates with our spirit and reveals God's heart to us. Revelation from this Spirit-to-spirit communion bubbles up into our senses so that our brain can process what God is saying. Inner knowing is sensing what God is saying without hearing through words or pictures. It is just the sense or feeling that God wants us to do something, pray for someone, or just that He is answering a question. We have what people call a kind of 'gut feeling.'

We will often miss the inner knowing if we are not aware that this intuition or 'gut feeling' is from God. We can second-guess the message thinking it is just human intuition. We need to pay attention, as with the other senses, and ask Holy Spirit if it is His intuition, and then act accordingly. We cannot assume that every feeling or intuition we have is from God, but some will be. As we agree with God and use discernment, more and more of our hunches or gut feelings will be from God.

We grow in discernment or understanding of whether the feeling we have is a God feeling or our own feeling as we spend time with God each day. God will give us discernment over time as we trust Him and take a step of faith and test these unctions.

Our Spiritual Senses

Just as babies learn to experience the natural world through five senses of sight, sound, taste, touch, and smell, God has given us spiritual senses with which we learn to experience Him and the spiritual world. The spiritual senses of seeing, hearing, taste, touch, and smell are excellent tools for communing with God.

For many people, either hearing God's voice through thoughts in their minds or seeing God pictures is their usual way to understand what God is communicating. When babies begin to communicate and understand the language of those around them we call that their first language. As children grow, they are capable of learning other languages so that they are proficient with their first language but have the ability to speak and understand second, third, and even more natural languages. Likewise, with spiritual communication, we can learn to hear God through more than one language.

For example, even if hearing or vision is not our first language, we can learn these languages in order to better understand God. We can recognize the importance of seeing (spiritual vision) and hearing God's voice as important ways of understanding what our Heavenly Father wants because Jesus used these methods while He was here on earth[7].

Seeing

The Bible tells us to fix our eyes on Jesus and to follow His example of looking to see what His Father was doing. Jesus answered;

> *I tell you the truth, the Son can do nothing by himself. He does only what he sees the Father doing. Whatever the Father does, the Son also does. For the Father loves the Son and shows him everything he is doing. In fact, the Father will show him how to do even greater works than healing this man. Then you will truly be astonished.*[8]

The Bible also tells us some of the benefits of spiritual vision:

- that the eyes of your heart may be flooded with light (Ephesians 1:18) so we can understand the confident hope that is our inheritance

- that your eyes may always be on the Lord for He rescues you from the traps of your enemies (Psalm 25:15)

- to reveal or prophesy of things to come (Revelation 1:1)

- to impassion you to run your race with endurance, stripping off any entanglements of sin. (Hebrews 12:1-2)

- Spiritual vision is the reward for the pure in heart (Matthew 5:8)

- Revelations bring understanding and instruction (2

7 John 5:19–20
8 John 5:19,20

Corinthians 12:1-7)

I have found that using the eyes of my heart to see is very valuable in hearing the voice of God through my internal sense of 'hearing'. Each morning as I spend time with Jesus, I ask Holy Spirit to show me where Jesus is with me. Holy Spirit gives me a sense as to where Jesus is around me. I then focus my attention on where the Spirit has told me and begin to see with my inner eye where He is. The way I see Him also shows me what He wants to talk about. For example, when Holy Spirit directs me to see Jesus in my kitchen, Jesus often speaks to me about the Scriptures; this either teaches me a new concept that I may teach others, or some fresh truth to edify, correct or train me in righteousness. After all, the Scriptures are spiritual food that strengthens my life!

Activation: If we are not natural seers (those for whom picturing is the way they receive from God), we can learn to see visions. We can 'oil the wheels' or 'prime the pump' of vision by opening our inner eyes (eyes of our hearts) and picturing with our imagination what the Lord will show us. Following are steps that may be necessary to overcoming obstacles to seeing visions and dreaming God-given dreams.

- We need to repent for unbelief and for cursing our vision with words like "I can't" or "I never dream or see visions."

- We may need to repent for looking at images (e.g. horror movies, sexually explicit pictures) that have damaged or marred our imaginations.

- To open our spiritual vision we need to know it is biblical to look, as shown in Revelation 1:10-12 and 4:1-2. Remember, while Jesus was here on earth He looked into the spiritual realm (into heaven) to see what His Father was doing, then did it[9].

- You can exercise your spiritual vision and cleanse it by meditating and picturing passages of Scripture like

---

9 John 5:19

Psalms 1, 23, and 91[10] as well as any of the visions of the prophets[11] and the scenes from the gospels where Jesus was ministering[12].

- We need to dedicate our imaginations and spiritual vision to God. You may want to use the following prayers or pray in your own words.

Prayer of Repentance:

"Lord Jesus, I repent for using my imagination to dwell on, the eyes of my heart to see, and my ears to hear, ungodly things. I ask You to forgive me for anything I have taken into my eyes, ears, and imagination that has been sinful or offensive to You. I forgive myself for seeing, hearing, or imagining sinful material. I receive Your forgiveness. Amen."

Dedication Prayer:

"Thank You, Lord Jesus, for Your example of doing what You saw Your Father do. I purpose by Your power now to use the eyes of my heart and my imagination to honour You. I dedicate to You my imagination and my visual capacities and all of my senses. Thank You for the dreams You give to educate me in the night. I give You permission to activate my senses, to use my imagination, and to give me dreams. Amen."

Hearing

John 10:27 tells us that God's sheep hear His voice, He knows them, they follow Him, and nothing can pluck them out of His hand. For some, hearing God's voice happens easily and spontaneously and they naturally learn to recognize the still,

---

10   Focus on a vivid illustration like the trees and chaff in Psalm 1; Picture the Shepherd with whom you walk, as described in Psalm 23; with the eyes of your heart see Psalm 91's images of the shelter found in the promise of the Most High.
11   Imagine partaking in the experience of a prophet's vision such as that in Ezekiel 1.
12   Place yourself in one of the Gospel accounts of Jesus' ministry. Imagine being a bystander in Luke 5:11 or a witness of Matthew 8:14–15.

small voice; hearing God through words or thoughts is their first language. For many others, hearing and discerning the voice of God through words or thoughts must be learned and practiced. As the Scriptures teach, God's sheep can and do hear His voice so we can be assured it is God's will to listen for His voice.

While at times God will interrupt our daily activities to speak in a particular moment, it is also wonderful to hear from Him continually, throughout the day, because we choose to tune in to His still small voice as described in 1 Kings 19:11-13. We stay connected to our Father in this way, known as practicing the presence of Christ, or referred to as praying without ceasing (something that would be impossible to do if we were the ones doing all the talking!)

Through the 1 Kings Scripture, we discover what God's voice sounds like most of the time, a 'still small voice' or, put another way, spontaneous thoughts that just pop into our minds. God's voice sounds like our thoughts but they are much wiser, more loving, and kinder than our thoughts. They are thoughts we have not been thinking and do not involve the intentional use of our own brain power. God speaks through our minds but not from our minds. He communes Spirit- to-spirit and His communication bubbles up through our spirit into our minds as thoughts so that we can hear His voice, respond to Him, and know Him.

A cool example of hearing God through His still small voice is that of Johannes Brenz, a Lutheran reformer, who was warned by an 'inner voice' of the approach of the Spanish army at Stuttgart. The inner voice told him to go to a certain building in the upper city, find an open door, enter it, and hide under the roof. He obeyed, found the door, and hid as the voice had said. His hiding place was visited by a hen that daily laid two eggs for him until the danger was past. Isn't it great how God can look after us...and also answers the old question: Why did the chicken cross the road? To get Johannes crack'n!! But seriously, we may one day be in a situation that needs God's protection and provision and if we can hear God well He can give us the 'heads up' like Mr. Brenz had so many centuries ago.

You may also use questions to help with focusing your inner ears on hearing from God. For example, each morning I begin my day by asking God what He would like to say to me. Then I quiet myself, picture Jesus (by asking the Holy Spirit where Jesus is with me), and tune in to the inner thoughts and words that begin to flow. I write down what I have sensed God say, then when I am finished listening and writing, I discern and judge if I have heard God by comparing it to God's character and His principles given in the Bible. Hearing God through journaling His voice is a subject addressed later in this book.

Music: Another way God can speak to us through our auditory sense is by music. Many hear God through this language, not only through the words of a song but also through the sound of the music, beat, rhythm, and melody. In fact, I have had several clear words from God through music on the radio at the moment I was asking God a question. I have even heard God through the songs of birds!

Taste, Touch, and Smell

As we have said, God's language can come through all of our senses and often grows as we spend more time listening and waiting on Him. Like any friendship, friendship with God gets closer the more time we spend with Him. Holy Spirit will at times expand our language through the use of taste, touch, and smell. These senses can be noticed individually or come as a multi-sensory experience where vision and hearing may be involved.

We have found that taste, touch, and smell may be used as confirmation of something God has been speaking to us about already. When they happen on their own, these senses need interpretation. The fragrance of the Lord, for example, has brought me and many others into the awareness of God's presence with them in their quiet times with Him as well as occasions when assurance[13] of His nearness is

13   Covered in detail in *The Language of Dreams and Visions* under the Dictionary of Symbols – Body Parts.

needed. Another example of the sense of smell...I experienced smelling the scent of oranges when praying for a young couple. This smell told me that they had a sweet fruitfulness around them. I felt God tell me through inner knowing that they were kind and gracious to others and their ministry was fruitful for God.

The sense of touch could happen by God's touch, perhaps on your hand, which would mean He is talking about your direction or work. We may also experience the presence of God by feeling the weight of His presence or the kabod as it is called in Hebrew.

An example of interpreting the sense of taste would be the taste of honey representing the sweet presence of God. As scripture says, Jesus Christ is sweeter than honey. Once again, testing revelation of this kind is essential as well as taking into account the context of when and where these things are taking place.

Suggested Journaling Exercises

Thank You Lord, that You are speaking to me and for the ability to know Your voice. Please speak to me about the language you have already given to me.

Write down or draw in your journal all the Lord communicates to you.

Lord, speak to me about how I can grow in hearing Your voice.

Write down or draw in your journal all the Lord communicates to you.

The Faith Factor
The Key That Unlocks Supernatural Life

Without faith it is impossible to please God, because anyone who comes to Him must believe that He exists and that He rewards those who earnestly seek Him[14].

It is by faith that we step into God: without knowing all the answers, we believe God and move forward. Just as we come into relationship with the Godhead by putting our trust in the price Jesus Christ paid for our sin, we step into all of the benefits of knowing Him by faith.

---

14   Hebrews 11:6

What is Living By Faith?

We could answer what it is to live by faith by examining how life looks when we do not act in faith. It is possible to believe in Jesus, but not live by faith. We can believe in theory yet live a natural lifestyle. Our decisions are based on human reasoning and human resources. We would not live beyond what we can accomplish through our abilities.

Often people will pray for God's wisdom but don't believe He will speak personally to them. They continue on in their own understanding, reasoning, and assessment of their situation. They hope for the best and ask God to bless what they decide to do.

We can go our entire lives assuming we are living by faith in the lifestyle I've mentioned – in fact, I did just that for twenty years! However, faith without works (action) is dead[15]. Real active faith comes from believing He has the best plan. Faith waits for God to give the plan and then does what it senses God is directing. Of course, God can and does intervene to change, direct, and correct our course, even though we may not listen to Him. His grace covers many of our mistakes. Active faith assumes God is interested, listening, and will not only communicate His desire to us but direct and manage the outcome of each facet of practical living.

An example of faith without action (which is what the Bible calls dead) would be my relationship with the Prime Minister of Canada. I opted, through citizenship, to become a Canadian. I have a healthy fear of and appreciation for the Prime Minister. I obey, to the best of my abilities, the laws of his dominion and read his comments or watch and listen to his broadcasts. I may actually like the Prime Minister but I really do not love him or communicate with him personally. Though I would not break the laws of the land he rules, I never expect him to take part in my personal decisions or imagine that I could talk over with him my plans and desires. This is close to what my relationship with God was like for many years of my Christian life. The outcome of this

---

15   James 2:26

kind of faith without action is that one can only accomplish what human resources can achieve. There will be little supernatural accomplishment when we live this way because we will only do what our reasoning and resources allow.

I have heard a radio preacher teaching his audience that the will of God is a bit like a football field in that it is large and encompassing. He taught that when we need to make a decision, like who to marry for example, we need not be concerned about knowing exactly which person is God's specific choice. He said anyone in the field who met the criteria (of a good Christian) would be an equally acceptable choice to God. I have to disagree most strongly. God has specific choices of our life partner and many other directions He desires us to take. He is well able to communicate and direct us to those choices if we will pay attention and allow Him to. God has a history of being very specific in scripture; we only need look at the specifications He gave Moses for the temple to realize God has very particular plans and intentions. I believe God loves us so much that His interest in us is even more intense than the colours in the Old Testament temple. Bible characters were guided to their life partners in very specific ways, so why would He not want to guide us specifically?

Hearing God for specific direction takes faith in action. It demands more of us, a deeper life of communion with Jesus than the football field approach, but it is in the deeper more intimate relationship with God that true satisfaction and supernatural living is found.

Faith In Action:

Someone who is living a life of faith grows in practicing the presence of Jesus Christ. Just as in any healthy relationship communication comes from both parties. Each one knows what the other likes and dislikes. The communication grows deeper as more time is given to it, even to the point of understanding what the other's inner desires, hopes, and future plans involve. The relationship is one of love and commitment where each person becomes vitally interested in and mutually relies on the other. When faith is lived out, the two - the individual person and God - become one. The person lives in union with God, not deciding or planning without first listening to God, which is made possible by the indwelling presence of Holy Spirit.

Spirit-to-spirit connection with God is the birthright of every born-again believer! This life of union with God is similar to an excellent, loving, marriage. Each partner is living in daily loving communication with the other. Each one honours the personhood of the other, desiring only the best, and acting with respect toward each other. Their life is shared and the relationship gives birth to joint hopes, desires, and plans. This is what faith in action looks like. Here in our earthly lives, God has made it possible to enjoy divine union with Himself by the connection of our human spirit with His Holy Spirit.

It is only possible to live our lives in union with God by His power and on His terms.

Galatians 2:20 gives us a glimpse of what this encompasses:

> *My old self has been crucified with Christ. It is no longer I who live, but Christ lives in me. So I live in this earthly body by trusting in the Son of God, who loved me and gave himself for me.*

A dead person cannot make decisions, evaluate with their own reason, or act on any impulse, desire, or need. Though we are not physically dead (in our dead-to-self-yet-alive-in-God state,) we choose to yield our human resources to the divine nature -our spirit made one with Holy Spirit.

By faith we live our new life, following the lead of the indwelling Holy Spirit. We live through His direction, power, and love by choosing to turn to Him and not our own resources. This yielded life fulfills God's purposes and brings Him glory, enabling Him to accomplish impossible supernatural things through our lives[16].

---

16   Mark 9:29

Jesus, Our Example:

Jesus is the perfect example of a life lived in union with God. Jesus came to earth in human form so He could show us the possibilities and potential we have when we live in connection with the Holy Spirit. While here on earth, Jesus limited Himself to the same resources we all are given but He also had the faith of God. His faith put into action healings, miracles, and signs in the earth. This same power that lived in Jesus Christ is now living in us. Stepping into this life of active faith is our choice. Faith comes from God and is increased by God. As we trust and take risks, He meets us and proves He is trustworthy. Faith grows by experiencing the faithfulness of God to deliver what He wants to do in and through us. Our part is to turn to God in faith and believe what He says. As we act on His direction we will experience the supernatural life of Christ in us. The following prayer will position you to allow God to work greater active faith in your soul.

Thank You, Father, Son, and Holy Spirit; You are my God. I have no other resource that can compare with You. Today I give myself to you and ask that You give me the kind of faith that pleases You. I ask for faith to hear You more clearly and to do as You ask. I ask for boldness to step out into Your plans. Help me in my weakness, Lord, and deliver me from all fear and concern. I yield to Your desires and plans because You love me. You have good plans, hope, and a good future for me. I trust You today to increase my ability to believe and follow You.

In Jesus' name, Amen.

Stop, Look & Listen
Hearing God Through Journaling

People who heard God's voice in the Bible heard Him through words, pictures, visions, dreams, through nature, and in many other ways. There are prophets in the Bible who were very good at hearing God and one of them tells us exactly how he did it. In Habakkuk 2:1-4 the prophet is describing how he could hear God. At the time, he was upset because he felt God was letting the Babylonians do evil to his people. He wants an answer from God so he tells us what he did.

> *I will climb up to my watchtower and stand*
> *at my guardpost. There I will wait to see what*
> *the Lord says and how he[a] will answer my*
> *complaint. Then the Lord said to me, "Write my*

answer plainly on tablets, so that a runner can carry the correct message to others. This vision is for a future time. It describes the end, and it will be fulfilled. If it seems slow in coming, wait patiently,   for it will surely take place. It will not be delayed. Look at the proud! They trust in themselves, and their lives are crooked. But the righteous will live by their faithfulness to God."

First, Habakkuk had to stand still and focus or **stop** what he was doing and pay attention. Next, He watched or **looked** to see what God would say...wait a minute...do you look to hear? I think it is more common to look to see but we do hear much better what is actually being said if we look and hear together. We see that Habakkuk **listened** very carefully. He says in that verse that he will wait and learn the answers to his questions so he is not going to have a quick listen and run off. He is going to take the time to wait and learn. Then in verse two God tells him to write the message clearly on tablets so it will be easy to read. God says to be patient and wait for the things He says are going to happen because it will take some time. In verse four He tells Habakkuk what to do with the message...let others know and the wise will listen, but some will not and those will be beyond help.

Three Simple Steps to Hearing God's Voice through Words

As has been said, God wants to speak to us which He does in many ways. People often need language to solidify and understand concepts, so it is very helpful if we learn to hear God through words. Following are three simple steps to help you hear and then record what God is telling you. First we need to **stop**, next we need to **look**, and then **listen**. As we listen to God it is best to write down what we hear so we can keep listening and remember everything He says. These three words are a reminder of how to connect with God at any time. Hearing God is simple - childlike in fact. So let's come to Him in childlike faith believing in His desire for us.

Step 1: Stop
Way back in history people realized if they wanted to hear God they needed to slow down, stop talking, and listen up! They gave it the name of 'stillness'. Being still to know God was practiced by the men and women in the Bible and is mentioned many times. Following are some Bible references which tell us to be quiet, listen to God and meditate on His response: Psalm 2: 1-3, Psalm 27: 14, Psalm 37: 7, Psalm 131: 2, Proverbs 1: 33, Isaiah 40: 29, Hosea 2: 14, Matthew 11: 28-30, Luke 10: 39, Hebrews 4: 9-11.

Becoming still is the process of quieting yourself. We need to quiet the noise around us and within us. We have so many distractions in our lives that we have to make a concentrated effort to stop the noise and be still. Following are some common distractions and how to deal with them.

Allow time: As you learn to relax and meet with God you will need to dedicate some time to the process. Clock-watching is a distraction which can be removed by setting a timer. Give yourself time to settle into stillness, then some time to listen to God and write down what He is saying. I have found about 30 minutes is a good length of time to begin. As you grow in your times with God it is very easy to spend an hour or more with Him in this focused way. Of course, we need to remember that God is always with us but very often we are not present with Him and attentive to His voice.

Remove outer distractions: Find a place where you will not be disturbed by electronic devices, phones, or the movement of other people or pets. Things you may need are a pen, notepad, a glass of water, and, if you are planning a longer period of time, you may need a pillow and blanket.

Make yourself physically comfortable - find a restful position. If you lay down, choose a position that is different from your normal sleeping position or guess what will probably happen! For those who feel most relaxed while walking, choose a quiet, solitary place to walk where you can easily relax and focus on God.

Remove inner distractions: Relax, smile a little. You may want to whisper the name of Jesus several times to focus your thoughts. Perhaps you will not need any further steps before you begin to sense God.

For some, however, this is when the mind begins to flit about or go into activity. Stillness of mind is not emptying the mind of thoughts but quieting the mind to focus on the presence of Jesus. Don't try to force your mind to be quiet or it probably will try harder to get you thinking. Just listen to the thoughts and see what the issue is. You can ask Holy Spirit, "What are my thoughts?" He will show you. Here is a list of things that cloud our thoughts.

- Worry: Give the worry over to God in prayer. Tell Him you trust Him to hold the issue (or person) during your time together. Picture the concern in God's hands and command worry to be silent in the name of Jesus.

- The to-do list: Just write the list down as your mind will feel better knowing you got the message and you will get to the list later.

- People to pray for: Even friends in need of prayer must be put on hold for the time being. Just make a note of the names and choose to pray for them later. This is your time to personally connect and hear God's heart for you. Don't let any other need take away from your time with Him.

- Sin-consciousness: Guilt can be a barrier to meeting with God. God has provided the ultimate help for us through Jesus. He has more than paid for our sin with His life given on the cross. Just bring your sin to Him and agree with Him for your cleansing and restoration. Receive your forgiveness. Allow Him to wash over you in loving acceptance. As the Bible says, there is no condemnation or separation for God's people. We are welcome to the Father's throne of grace and nothing can separate us from His love.

Remember that condemnation, guilt, and shame are not sent from God. He takes you as you are. By His precious blood, you are now fully accepted into His family as His child and heir. It is now your inheritance to fully enjoy your Father, and for Him to fully enjoy time with you.

The right attitude: Thankfulness and worship (admiration for God and His ways) is the doorway to God's zone. Have faith that God wants to talk to you even more than you want to talk to Him. He is looking forward to sharing thoughts with you and helping you to know Him.

Repent of any negative words: Pray a simple prayer to renounce any negative words that may have hindered you from hearing God. Words such as, "I can't hear God", "God doesn't talk to me" or "Who do you think you are? You can't hear God." Forgive anyone who has said negative words over you. Ask forgiveness for saying and believing that you do not hear God. Receive your forgiveness for any sin that may be disturbing your ability to come to God. Repent for wrong use of your hearing (for example: listening to negative, anti- God, swear words or music). Dedicate your inner ears to God.

Step 2: Look

It is so much easier to understand what a person really means if we can see them. Texting is not the best way of communicating because although it is a fast, almost instant way to talk you can easily misunderstand the message. Misunderstandings happen when we can't see the expressions and hear the tones of people. There is something important about multi-sensory communication that helps us to hear. The prophets used vision and hearing to get God's message. Jesus only did what He saw his father do[17] and so we can use the eyes of our hearts and our inner ears as we listen to God. The Bible also tells us to fix our eyes on Jesus[18] so using our inner eyes to picture Jesus is biblical and very helpful.

Picturing Jesus: You may ask Holy Spirit where Jesus is in the room with you then focus on His presence. Or you could picture yourself in a comfortable scene with Him,

17   John 5:19
18   Hebrews 12:12

perhaps putting yourself into a Bible scene like being with Jesus at the Sea of Galilee.

Step 3: Listen

Ceasing from activity (both outward and inwardly) and quieting ourselves before God allows us to listen. Often, when people are learning to hear God, they need to 'oil the wheels' of the inner ears by asking a question.

Some questions you could use are: "How do You see me, God?" or "What do You want to say to me about hearing Your voice, (seeing You, being with You)?" "Jesus speak to me about my friendship with You."

Every morning I begin my day with the question, "What do You want to say to me today, Lord?"

Keep your question simple and open-ended so that you will not be receiving a yes or no answer. God desires to spend time with you and commune with you. Yes or no answers shorten the conversation and are difficult to test. The Lord wants relationship with you and getting to know His heart for you means spending time listening and talking together. You can follow these steps to help you to hear God's voice.

1. Picture Jesus: Begin by using the eyes of your heart (your imagination) to picture being with Jesus. Often people find it easier to become childlike seeing themselves as a young child in a well-known scene (for me it is the beach as I grew up as a child spending much time on the beach in Australia).

2. Ask your question: Choose any of the questions mentioned previously and wait for flowing spontaneous thoughts or pictures to come.

3. Write down the conversation: It is good to keep a journal of your time with God including dreams, visions, and God's words to you. Date each conversation or God encounter so you can test and re-read them at a later date.

4. Test what you have heard: When we are learning a new

skill, we usually need a mentor or teacher who is good at the thing we are trying to learn. The advice of more experienced friends will help us grow and stay on track in the new skill of hearing and understanding God's voice. It is a wonderful encouragement and support to have several trusted friends who can help, reassure and show you how to test what you have written or experienced. Ask people who are mature in their faith, already hear God well, that you feel safe sharing with, and who are encouraging and kind.

5. Confirmation: You can always ask God to give you confirmation for anything you are unsure of. I have often been given Scripture references (just the book of the Bible and the numbers) which, when I found them in the Bible, confirmed what God had been speaking to me in my time of listening.

Journal Exercise

Write a letter to God telling Him how you feel about Him, then picture yourself with Jesus and ask Him one of these questions: How do you see me Jesus? Or talk to me about my friendship with you, God... Write what you feel, the thoughts that come as well as what you see below your note to God.

Use no more than a few lines of your journal to talk to Him and then use a page for His answer to you.

Discerning Direction
Knowing Which Signs to Follow

By faith, we can move mountains (Jesus tells us) so we can certainly hear God by putting our faith in His ability to speak loud enough for us to hear. I have explained already what I mean by 'hearing God'. He speaks not only through words but also in many other ways. We need to become attentive to the fact that God wants to guide and direct us and when we ask him a question He will send us the answer. Often God will answer in several ways so that we can be sure of what He is saying.

Keeping Your Antenna Up:

When asking God for direction, know He is keener on giving you guidance than you realize. We often ask and then forget to look and listen for the answer. If we are attentive we will receive several incoming revelations. Listening for God's direction as we live our everyday life is a skill God wants each of us to acquire. If we believe God has the best plan and He loves us, we will be excited to hear from Him each day.

If we ask Him to keep us attentive to His voice we will begin to notice how many ways He is speaking. As we practice listening each day we learn to be more confident about the bigger questions of life. For example, perhaps we have asked God a directional question. He may answer by giving us a dream. We need to interpret the dream through journaling and pondering it. As we go about our day a friend may offer some words that agree with your sense of God's direction from the dream. This will add to the revelation. You could also have a financial blessing that would help cover the possible costs. Perhaps as you research some practical aspects of your potential decision you see some possibilities that encourage you to begin to take a step. You may even see a sign in the natural that Holy Spirit highlights to you giving you another nudge in the same direction. The biggest help will be to keep a journal of your questions and then remember to keep your spiritual antenna up ready to receive.

Agreement

We are often able to enlist the help of fellow believers who also have faith that God speaks and directs. I have many times asked people on the team involved in my ministry to soak and pray with me about the direction God has for a particular situation. Agreement is a wonderful tool in knowing what God is saying. When two or more are gathered together in agreement to hear God He definitely comes and helps us[19]. We most surely need the agreement of those our decision will directly involve. For example, if we are feeling God prompting

---

19   Matthew 18:20

us to move our family, we need to ask the adults in the family to consult Him. Then compare what they feel He is saying with what you have. Even children can be involved in this process as long as they don't feel worried or fearful of the move (in which case it is better to just seek the Lord and then work with the children to ease their fears).

In my experience, agreement has been a wonderful help in knowing God's will. My husband and I often practice listening prayer asking God the same question or presenting the same topic to Him. When we both feel we have His answer we compare what we feel God has said to us. When our revelation agrees we act on it. When we do not have matching answers or complementary revelation, we wait. Perhaps the timing is not right. We may need more pieces of this plan to fall into place so we will have a smooth transition into the plan. After some time has passed, if the idea has not taken form or more revelation has not formulated, we do not move ahead into it. The proposal was not God and so we let go of the idea, being thankful that God rescued us from a mistake.

Confirmation

I always ask God for confirmation if a direction changing question is involved. In fact, He often gives more than one confirmation. Confirmation often comes to me through Scripture. I know God would not want me to go against scripture so the decision must be in agreement with Biblical principles. He often gives me a verse which may even contain the same words that God has given in the journaling I had recorded.

God loves to confirm through people, even those who don't realize you are asking a question. Many times I have heard messages over the media, read signs or articles as well as hearing a confirming message in church.

Circumstances also begin to align around us. For example, we might receive a job offer, promotion, or some other form of opportunity that enables us to move toward the direction we were praying about.

If no answer comes, even though you have been listening and watching attentively, then perhaps the timing is not right and God is saying wait.

God wants us to be in the centre of His will so if you are not sensing His momentum toward the direction you had asked about I advise not to push ahead. God opens doors we do not have to push. Remember the scripture: God opens doors no one can shut and shuts doors no one can open[20]. If we have to push, it is probably not a God opening. God has used all of these ways to reaffirm His direction in my life. The more we expect to be guided by Him (which is really faith in action) the more usual it will be that we hear from God and discern His direction.

Suggested Journal Exercise

Holy Spirit, please speak to me about being attentive to your voice.

Write down or draw in your journal all the Lord communicates to you.

---

20   Revelation 3:7

Christian Meditation
Using the Grey Matter & More

Christian meditation is the ancient practice of focusing the mind on one simple concept and letting God expand and explain it[21]. Our goal is to slow down to connect with God. Meditation focuses our mind and senses so that we can make truth part of our thinking and change our perspective to God's perspective. As we give God our time and attention, the Holy Spirit shows us God's view, helping us to agree with the mind of Christ (which is alive within us). Our minds and hearts need this time and attention to adjust to God's

---
21   Canadian Oxford Dictionary

perspective. As we meditate on God and His word He gives us His understanding, with which comes peace and calm.

Christian meditation uses the soul (mind, will, emotions, imagination, and conscience) to connect with God and truly understand what He is saying. Eastern religion's meditation involves emptying the mind and overcoming the pain of uncomfortable meditation positions by relaxation techniques. Christian meditation is very different because it focuses attention on God and His word which fills and refuels our lives. This process of meeting with and 'hearing' God allows God's thoughts to go deep, becoming part of us so that we can recognize where adjustments need to be made. Meditation gives God the Spirit freedom to move truth to a deeper level within us so that truth changes us. Our minds are renewed by the truth as God moves through our soul.

Taking in the truth is more effective when our mind, will, emotions, conscience, and imagination are involved, which is what Christian meditation does. Being focused but relaxed, as well as slowing down our thoughts, helps us to take in what God's Spirit is teaching us. More is learned than just the work of study which only involves the mind through human reasoning, leaving out all the other parts of our soul.

The process of Christian meditation on Scripture, for example, is similar to memorization with the added benefit of inviting the flow of Holy Spirit. We do this not to get the words exact in the mind, then to use human reasoning to think about the meaning, but to include Holy Spirit's explanation and expansion of the words. Meditation invites Him to interact with our senses, bringing the scripture or topic alive. To properly take in spiritual food we must slowly think over and over (chew well) the thoughts and words of God and let our inner man feed on the things God wants to teach us. It is a bit like cows chewing their grass over and over. As the grass moves through their stomachs cows get every bit of nutrition from it. As we meditate or think over and over with the Holy Spirit's help, we receive all God is saying to us at that time, not just the quick surface information that our own thoughts can come up with.

For example: When we use our reasoning abilities to think through a scripture we begin at point A, which examines the whole passage or verse. Through a process of study, as well as research, we break down the information within the passage and decide what it is telling us. B may be some insight which will cause us to research other things. C will lead us to D, E and so on until we reach our conclusion at Z. This way of examining the scripture, studying, is rather like a straight line or linear thinking as below.

A • B • C ••• Z

A through Z until conclusion is reached.

The meditative process looks quite different. We begin at the same point (A), examining the passage or verse, but instead of only using the reasoned approach of studying and researching, we apply what I call circular thinking. Meditation uses our brain but not to logically study. The brain is used to repeat scripture over and over so our soul can receive thoughts and impressions from Holy Spirit. As we begin reading or replaying the whole passage several times at first, we gradually narrow down our focus to fewer and fewer words or fragments of scripture. A picture of this process would look like a spiral where Z is at the centre.

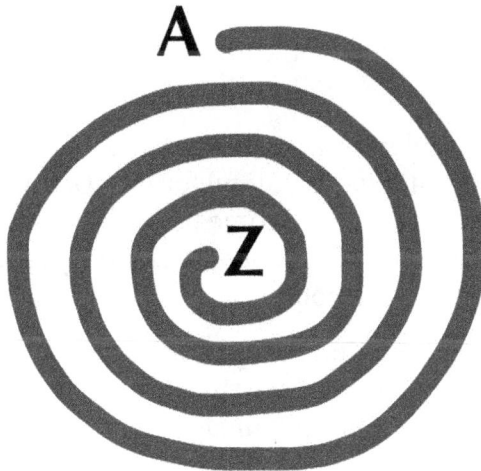

The spiral creates smaller and smaller circles as it

moves in toward the centre. This represents fewer words repeated and focused on. As we ponder fewer words more of the meaning is made known to us at a deeper level because the Holy Spirit is teaching us. The meditative process is like spiritual digestion. The truth becomes part of our inner-man and is emphasized or detailed by the senses (visions, taste, touch, scents, words or scriptures and emotions).

It is best to start with just one concept or verse at a time. If we do choose larger passages, be prepared to take several sessions to complete your meditation. Slowing down and focusing on fewer words is more helpful than trying to take in a whole chapter at one time.

Simple Steps for Biblical Meditation

Become Still
Quieting yourself is a process of first removing, as much as possible, any outer distractions such as:

- • Time: Set a time to avoid the distraction of clock watching.

- • People: Let friends or family who may interrupt you know you are having some God time.

- • Telephone and electronic interruptions: Devices need to be off. You can't text and meditate! Sorry

- • Be comfortable: Pain can distract you. You do not have to be physically still if it is painful for you. Our aim is to focus on the Bible passage and some people find moving helps them to focus. I've known people to meditate while they jog or do laps in the pool.

Once you have time, people, quiet and comfort looked after, move your attention from the outer body to quieting the soul (mind, will, emotions, imagination, and conscience). Perhaps you will not need any further steps before you begin to sense God. I have found if we use the mind in meditating on Scripture and the imagination through picturing that the emotions and will usually come along for the ride. Sometimes our conscience is reminded we have sinned. If we just confess our sins God will forgive us and we can quickly move on. Don't let guilt bother you. Jesus died so you can be free to be with God so tell guilt to go and focus on God again. Following is a list of things you can do to help you settle inwardly. You may like to try one of these:

Calling on the Name of Jesus:
If we call on the name of Jesus He will answer and meet with us. You may want to whisper the name of Jesus several times to focus your thoughts. You may pray the simple Jesus prayer which many people through the ages have prayed to focus their attention: "Lord Jesus Christ have mercy upon me." This prayer is softly and slowly spoken (or thought) till you sense the presence of Jesus. Relax. You are calling the Lover of your soul, your heavenly Parent, who dearly desires to spend time with you.

Picturing Jesus:
I often picture Him with me by asking the Holy Spirit where Jesus is with me. When I sense where Jesus is I then focus my attention on Him, thanking and worshiping Him. Then, allow the Spirit to take over and watch and listen to what happens. You can interact with Jesus about your meditation or just begin to slowly speak the words of scripture.

Connecting with Holy Spirit:
I turn my attention to Holy Spirit by offering praise and thanks to Him for His presence in my life. I focus upon His light within me giving Him permission to move upon all of my thoughts, senses, and emotions. I wait upon Him and then lift up the passage of scripture.

The Experience of Meditation:
Once you feel at peace and sense God's presence with you, gently turn your thoughts to the pre-selected topic or scripture for meditation. Record your starting point

(scripture, topic, question, or thought). Begin to ponder by applying circular thinking (the words repeated slowly over and over in the mind), pause between each repetition, rest in each repetition, linger, ponder, allowing time for God's interaction within each repetition.

Continue on the one thought or line of scripture until you sense a deepening of understanding. This may come in the form of:

- Vision: by way of mental pictures or inward videos.

- Thoughts: These interjected, spontaneous thoughts sound like you but are more; they are Holy Spirit's thoughts through you. They are much wiser bringing meaning and enlightenment.

- Flowing emotions: Sometimes our emotions are moved and we may feel joy and elation or tears may come. The emotions can also carry Father's feelings so that we can relate to His heart for us.

- Taste Touch and Smell: God created all of our senses so He may use them to communicate and deepen our understanding as He leads us into all truth through meditation.

Remember, without faith it is impossible to please God and we must come to God believing that He loves us and desires even more than we do to communicate and teach us[22]. We are told in the scriptures to meditate on His word day and night so our time is well spent and faith well invested as we allow Holy Spirit to take us deeper[23].

Journaling:
Record what is coming through words, thoughts, vision, or other senses. As we receive with thankfulness more will be given. Writing down or recording what is happening allows us the freedom to keep receiving, knowing we will be able to test and pray over the concepts and thoughts later. Feel free to ask God what He is saying or showing as it is happening.

22 Hebrews 11:6
23 Joshua 1:8

Interact with Him like you do with a close friend. After all, He already knows what you are thinking. As you give voice to your own thoughts, you are better able to process the communication flowing between you and God. Your clear questions will be met with His clear response and will give your mind a focal point for deeper meditation.

Conclusion

Worship and give thanks for the time together with God. Honour your heavenly Father for the revelation and time He shared with you. It is always good to go over your previous meditation so that you are in flow as you approach Him for the next conversation.

Through this simple process, I have found a deeper understanding of God's eternal Biblical truth which has enriched my personal walk of faith with Jesus. Before I understood the process of meditation I had a more limited understanding of the scriptures, even though I had read and memorized them for many years. Through the practice of meditation, my love for God and His written Word increased along with an understanding of His wisdom and counsel for everyday decisions. The Logos has in this way become personal revelation (Rhema)[24]. It has quickened my soul thus becoming part of who I am by aligning my life in practical ways to God's truth and will.

God is a wonderful communicator. His desire to commune is greater than ours and He is very good at removing our barriers. Once, when I was doubting my ability to hear God, He said to me, ``I can talk louder than you can listen, so don't worry." Our faith is key, but God is in the business of increasing our little faith. God will increase our faith to receive as we trust and spend time with Him.

Suggested Meditation Exercise:

Try meditating on Psalm 23. Choose a version you are comfortable with. You may already have it memorized so you can slowly repeat each verse in your head without having to

24   See Chapter 5 Hearing God Through Scripture.

read it. Allow your heart to settle on a part of each verse you feel God wants you to focus on. Then write down the new thoughts, pictures, feelings, or insights you have after each verse:

The Lord is my shepherd; I have all that I need.

Write down or draw in your journal all the Lord communicates to you.

He lets me rest in green meadows; he leads me beside peaceful streams.

Write down or draw in your journal all the Lord communicates to you.

He renews my strength. He guides me along right paths, bringing honour to his name.

Write down or draw in your journal all the Lord communicates to you.

Even when I walk through the darkest valley, I will not be afraid, for you are close beside me. Your rod and your staff protect and comfort me.

Write down or draw in your journal all the Lord communicates to you.

You prepare a feast for me in the presence of my enemies. You honour me by anointing my head with oil. My cup overflows with blessings.

Write down or draw in your journal all the Lord communicates to you.

Surely your goodness and unfailing love will pursue me all the days of my life, and I will live in the house of the Lord forever.

Write down or draw in your journal all the Lord communicates to you.

Application:

What message is God telling you through this meditation today?

Write down or draw in your journal all the Lord communicates to you.

Checking It Out
God? Satan? Or Just Wishful Thinking?

We test the revelation (what we have received through any of the "languages" God may use) by comparing it with the character and nature of the names of God. For example, if the revelation is in agreement with God's names, with His nature and character, we know it is from Him.

There are three possible sources of the spiritual messages we receive, no matter how the message comes to us. The sources are as follows: The Spirit of truth (God), human thinking or desires (human soul), or a lying spirit (demonic spirit). We begin our examination with that which is true, then examine the false and finally our own desires.

The Spirit of Truth or God's voice:

Holy Spirit is the source of revelation. If we listen to His voice, He will show us how to apply it in our day-to-day lives. Therefore, it is imperative that we have invited Him to dwell within our spirits and that we are spending time with Him each day, talking and listening to what He has to say.[25] He will guide us into all truth[26]. As we live in this daily communion with God, we learn to discern the voice of God by the inner peace or assurance of Holy Spirit and can confidently receive guidance and encouragement from Him.

Before we begin to examine revelation, we must be sure to receive Holy Spirit (the Spirit of Truth) by asking Him to cleanse us from all past shortcomings, mistakes, and unforgiveness of the faults of others. This cleansing is made possible because when Jesus died for us, He took all of our past and present faults; He died for all the sin of the world and has risen from the dead. It is the Spirit of Christ that comes to reside within our spirit. We need to renounce all other commitments and connections to any other god, anti-biblical world views, or idol so that we can honestly confess that we have no other gods beside Father, Son, and Holy Spirit. Holy Spirit is the one who can speak to us from within, assure us of truth and give discernment to know if what we are hearing are our own desires or a lying spirit rather than Him.

God's character and nature: The more we know God, the easier it is to discern His voice. The names given to God are a big clue to His character and nature or ways. Following is a list of names for the Father, Son, and Holy Spirit found in the Bible (this is not a complete list of the names of God, but will be of some help).

God the Father: Almighty, Fortress, Healer, Heavenly Father, Holy One, I AM, Judge, King of Kings, The Lord is there, Lord of Lords, God is Love, Mighty God, Most High, My Banner, My Glory and the Lifter of my head, My Peace, My Righteousness

---

25   Deuteronomy 30:20
26   John 14:12

God the Son: Lord Jesus Christ: Advocate, Almighty, Author and Finisher of our faith, Bread of Life, Captain of Salvation, Cornerstone, Creator, Day Spring, Deliverer, Desire of the Nations, The Door, Good Shepherd, Immanuel (God with us), King of kings, Lamb of God, Life, Light of the World, The Vine, The Truth, The Way God the Holy Spirit: Comforter, Counsellor, Fear of the Lord, Knowledge of God, the Spirit of Might, Our Guide, Peace, Spirit of Christ, Spirit of Holiness, Spirit of Truth, Wisdom, and Understanding

Lying spirits or Satan's voice:

We can discern the negative voice of the enemy fairly easily because it aligns with the names, nature, and fruit of our enemy. Listed below are some examples to assist you.

Names: The enemy of God, The Devil, Satan, Deceiver, Father of Lies, Serpent, Accuser, Murderer, Thief, Robber, and a fallen angel of light.

Nature: the enemy is prideful, boastful, arrogant, rude, selfish, unkind, greedy, and egotistical.

Fruit: Enemy revelation produces: sin, fear, disunity, depression, rage, low self-worth, pride, shame, guilt, condemnation, and loss of many kinds. It is important to test the revelation we receive as is stated in scripture[27]. We must not disregard or make light of prophecy. Prophecy is God's voice to us directly or through another person. However, we need to test and prove that the message is coming from the Spirit of God[28].

Aligning Revelation With Scripture:

Scripture is our guide for confirmation. When we compare the revelation with scripture, the Holy Spirit will reveal if it is compatible and in agreement with what God has already said. If the revelation you have received does not align with or contradicts what God has already said in the Bible, it is probably not God speaking.

27   1 Corinthians 14:29 and 1 Thessalonians 5:21
28   1 Corinthians 13:8–10

There is an example of this in the Bible: Balaam the prophet[29] accepted money to curse Israel, despite God's previous command not to do so. Because Balaam listened to the nation paying him to curse Israel, God intervened and set him straight through the words of a donkey. This drastic example would not have been necessary if Balaam had used discernment to align the request of the enemy of Israel with God's nature (God is Love[30], the one who blesses His people) [31]and what God had already spoken about blessing Israel. While Balaam did not have written scripture in his day we do, and can therefore use Scripture as a reference for what God has already said and to learn about His character.

Testing Revelation By the Fruit or Results:

At times, we can anticipate the outcome of an action or direction before we take it. We can, for example, tell whether it will lead to loving God, loving our neighbour, and bringing blessing and unity, or sowing division among people. Will the action bring us toward or away from blessing and love? At other times we will not fully realize the fruit or results until we have stepped out and the action actually comes to pass. We need wisdom and sensitivity to Holy Spirit to discern. We will eventually see and understand the results if the revelation brings positive outcomes. Actions resulting from godly revelation will increase the fruit of the spirit in our lives and the lives of those with whom we interact. (Galatians 5: 21-23)

How to Discern Our Inner Thoughts From God's Voice

Our cognitive (thought producing), rational mind works to make decisions and think or ponder by our active choice. When we want to hear from God about a choice or decision

29   Numbers 22:15–35
30   Deuteronomy 7:9; Psalm36:7; Psalm 42:8; Joel 2:13; Jonah 4:2; Romans 8:39; 1 John 2:5; 1 John 3:1–10; 1 John 4:6–8
31   Psalm 98:3; Romans 12:14

in our lives, we can sometimes allow our own feelings and desires to interfere with hearing God. In order to distinguish our own inner voice from that of God's we first need to submit our will to God. We are to position ourselves to accept His answer regardless of whether it is what we desire in a particular situation. As we spend more time with God, we learn to distinguish between our own thoughts and preferences and God's voice.

It is essential that we do not hold our own desires or opinions higher than God's will. We will not be able to hear or discern God's voice clearly if we are very passionate about receiving a certain answer. We will always hear what we want to hear if we have very strong feelings on a subject. In such a situation the answer we desire becomes too important and blocks God's answer.

In the example of the prophet Balaam[32], when he initially asked God about the offer of money to curse Israel, he received an answer which was certainly in line with God's character; God loves, blesses and favours His people. Because Balaam wanted in his heart to accept the money, he decided to check again and this time heard the answer he wanted to hear. The money changed Balaam's ability to discern clearly because his desire for money was stronger than his desire for God's will.

We need to be able to receive any answer God gives so we must take the time to move from a strong desire to fulfill our will to becoming neutral. By purposing to become neutral about decisions, we will accept God's divine choice. Only then will we be positioned to hear clearly from God. As we spend more time listening and talking with God, we learn His character. Knowledge of the character of God (His desire is to give us abundant life, and He will not withhold any good thing from us) helps to motivate us toward accepting His good, perfect and pleasing will. I often have to wait to ask God about a decision or for His will on a topic until my desire is submitted to God's answer, whatever it may be. Sometimes it takes time and prayer to be ready (in neutral mode) to hear what God wants and not to just hear what I want. The wait is

32   Numbers 22–24

always well worth it.

The Counsel of Others:

Another safeguard when discerning God's voice is to share your revelation with some trusted friends. We find safety in the counsel of many. I have several close and trusted friends who hear God well and when I am in need of advice I know they will take the time to go over what I feel God has revealed to me. I have done the same for others to bring reassurance and discernment. It is a blessing to find counsel with those who love God, are growing in their friendship with Him, and value listening to His voice.

Confirmation from God:

Just as a loving father will carefully instruct and guide us, God in His great patience and kindness will make sure we understand His communication to us. As we learn to discern the voice of God, God confirms what He wants us to know. When we are not receiving or perhaps not understanding His message He will show us in other ways.

For example, God may confirm an inner-knowing that we need to give a financial gift through a dream, through journaling of His voice, a scripture, or a prophetic word. Keep in mind that if we have no means to give, it might not be a message from God. I have an example. I felt I heard God tell me to give a friend some money. At the time I was in a prayer meeting and afterward, I planned to buy my family groceries. I had the urge to give to her and toward the end of the meeting she asked for prayer for a financial need. She did not state the amount needed but I had my confirmation. I had just enough money for my family's needs, however, I felt convicted to give my friend the money. It turned out to be the exact amount she needed. I continued on to the grocery store with what money I had left and was greeted at the door by another friend who gave me the exact amount I had given away. He had felt to repay money that I didn't even remember loaning him. God works in wonderful ways to confirm the promptings of His Voice.

Suggested Journal Exercise

God please speak to me about the importance of testing what I feel you are saying.

Write down or draw in your journal all the Lord communicates to you.

How Others Have Learned to Listen Up

The following stories are wonderful descriptions of individual journeys to knowing God and understanding His voice. Each is vastly different from the others and you will notice, these people have different first languages in hearing God. Perhaps their experiences will help you to recognize your own first language for hearing God's voice.

Bob's Adventure
Hearing God through Inner-Knowing and Signs

When Bob was a very young boy, his father and mother taught him the importance of helping those less fortunate than himself. Bob remembers a time at the zoo when his mother gave him an apple and a dime to give to another little boy who was playing there. Bob felt deeply confirmed in his young heart that this was right and good. This was the first time he had the feeling of knowing inwardly that God was somehow involved.

As Bob grew he had several supernatural encounters with darkness that he realized were evil. He asked to be protected and even though he really was not sure about the existence of God, he knew he needed help. Each time, he did indeed receive protection and peace.

As a young man, Bob decided to travel to Australia alone. His father warned him with the words: "Son, you have a tiger by the tail!" Little did he realize how true those words would become!

Before leaving, his grandmother encouraged Bob by telling him that if he was ever in danger he could secretly pray. No one need know, but God would be with him. Many times while travelling, Bob encountered dangers. Again and again he asked God to protect him and he was miraculously kept safe. Once, while travelling in Hawaii, Bob was in grave danger from some men who were bent on evil. Bob was made invisible and walked right passed them. He knew God was real. Though he could not explain what God was saying in words Bob would get a gut feeling or prompting to go to a place or do a thing which was usually proven to be a God feeling.

Bob finally came into friendship with Jesus Christ when he gave God his life in 1981. When Yvonne (wife) became a Christian she told him she was going to be with God in heaven when she died. She was sad when she told him this because, at that time, he did not want God in his life and he was not going to be with her there. Bob knew what she said was right. Just as sure as the first time he knew it was right to give to the little boy, now he knew Jesus was real and God was telling him to come home to Him. He remembered the many times His parents and grandparents had taught him the truth about God and realized it was what he needed in his life. Bob's life changed that night and it has been an interesting, exciting, and fun journey. Since that time Bob has had many encounters as he has listened to and acted on the sense of inner-knowing. He has found it is his prime way to hear God.

Bob has been prompted to drive from home to Toronto (almost two hours away) not knowing why. He followed the unction, which exit to take, turn after turn, until he came into a subdivision where he noticed a very worried looking woman at a bus stop. Bob felt God prompting him to ask her if he could help. Sure enough, the woman was in need of help. She had just newly arrived in Canada and was off to her first job interview. She had missed her bus and didn't know what to do. Bob offered to drive her and even though it could have been risky for her, she felt safe to get into the truck. Bob was able to get her to her interview just in time. As he left, Bob assured her God had good plans for her and then he headed for home, mission accomplished!

Bob has many wonderful stories to tell of how God has lead him and spoken through signs as well as inner knowing. Bob often has experienced unusual things in nature (fish falling from the sky) that are signs from God that answer specific questions and give direction to him. Perhaps someday he will record them in his own book. By the faith God gives Bob he has learned to act on the gut feelings or unctions. Because he has acted, he has found out how to discern when it is God and when it is wishful thinking. He has learned to test (see Discerning Direction chapter 4) the unction or gut feeling and to ask for confirmations when big decisions are to be made. Bob learned to journal God's voice so he can hear in words. He has been given open visions when praying for situations. God has been growing and stretching Bob so that he hears God in many more ways than he once could. It is all because he has a willing teachable heart and loves a faithful God.

Irene's Story
God Speaks through Pictures

I have always loved to write down my thoughts and daily activities ever since I was a young girl. Little did I know that this would become the main avenue that God would use to speak His words to me in my later years.

I came to know Jesus when I was 33 years old. As a young Mom of 2 girls, I needed to know what I believed about Jesus so I could teach them the truth. I began my walk with the Lord mainly through reading the Bible, going to Bible studies and writing down my thoughts and prayers. I didn't know that God spoke in any other ways until He began to draw my attention to situations in the natural and then give me a spiritual meaning in my understanding. I remember one day we had a clogged drain in our bathroom. My Dad, being a plumber, came to unclog it. God began to speak to me through that circumstance to share with me about how my own heart was clogged and it kept me from receiving His truth and love.

I began a healing journey with a small group of women where we shared our stories of our childhood and discovered where these blockages began. It was during this time that God began to bring pictures to my mind and then explain the meaning of them and how they applied to my life as I journaled. I felt uncomfortable sharing these at first because I didn't know anyone else that heard God in this way.

Doubt was often crouching at my door to say, "You're wrong or crazy to think this is God". I know now that this was the voice of the enemy because he desperately doesn't want us to hear God's voice.

As time went on and I continued to seek God to heal my heart, He began to use the metaphor of a butterfly. He shared that I was His little butterfly and He was in the process of transforming me into a brand-new creation. Over and over He would give me a picture, and then confirm it to me in a tangible way through a gift or words from another person.

One day I remember feeling very discouraged and stuck in my cocoon, believing that I would never be free of my past. In my morning quiet time, I asked God for an encouragement. I proceeded to my place of work at our church and felt prompted to clean out a cupboard in the kitchen. To my amazement, I discovered a beautiful hand-made quilted sheet with a picture of an apple blossom tree, cocoon, and a butterfly, accompanied by the words "Come out of your cocoon". My heart was beating a mile a minute as I went to ask the secretary where this incredible piece of artwork came from. She responded to me, "I have never seen that before. I think God created that just for you!" Talk about an encouragement!

That was the beginning of God confirming to me that I was hearing His voice. He continued to speak to me through the butterfly analogy many times and confirmed each time with a surprise gift. It became so evident to me that whenever I saw a butterfly, I knew God was saying, "I am here!"

It wasn't until I met Yvonne through ordering one of her amazing prophetic prayer blankets that I learned that I am a seer. She explained that seeing is my first language, how God speaks to me. I was so excited and wanted to learn more. Yvonne invited me to a soaking group at her home where we learned more ways to hear God's voice. I was hungry for even more. It was a perfect setting to practice sharing what I was seeing and to develop my gift. It is so exciting to be able to use this gift to encourage and pray for others.

I have been so blessed to be a part of a weekly soaking group where we dedicate focused time to be still and listen to God's voice and share His message with one another. It has been a time of maturing and healing for me.

Just recently God has opened up an amazing opportunity for me to partner with Yvonne in making prayer blankets. I feel like I was born for this. It is a dream come true to be able to use my gift of hearing God's voice to make "tents of meetings" to encourage others to seek Him too!

Randy's Journey
Listening to God's Voice

On February 18th, 1999 at approximately 10:30 in the morning I was sitting in my home office doing some graphics work. I was listening to a CD that had been given to me as a gift. Song after song played and God filled me with His love and presence. When the second last song, "I See the Light" played, I began to weep. A voice inside me said, "Gotcha!" I laughed a little as I finally realized I was listening to the voice of Jesus, the voice I had been hearing most of my life. God had spoken to me in a way that was very personal. He proceeded to download some things He wanted me to do. At the top of that list was sharing what had happened with my wife who had given her life to Jesus years earlier. Irene had been praying faithfully for my salvation. Another thing on God's list for me was to read His Word. A month later on my 41st birthday, I was given a Bible which I read with great hunger in three months.

     The pastor of the church we had just started attending, took me under his wing. We met regularly as I began my walk with God. The pastor helped me gain a firm foundation and we developed a close lifelong friendship. I learned he had an amazing gift of asking just the right questions. When I talked about different times in my life I would sometimes experience an internal trembling which I came to realize was God showing me His presence was with me. He had been with me throughout my life, and in some cases even saving it! I had begun my walk with God by running hard after Jesus. I used to say it felt like I was riding a wild stallion and hanging on tight!

     Within a couple of months, I attended a "Spiritual Freedom Weekend". Late on the Saturday night, I was baptized by Holy Spirit and again the trembling came, but on a much stronger scale. I was incredibly excited and could barely sleep that night. I now had Jesus as my friend and Holy Spirit inside to guide me daily. As the years passed I grew closer to God as I learned more about Him from those around me, by digging into His Word, and through my personal relationships with Spirit-filled friends and leaders.

The natural world has always fascinated me and I feel closest to God when in natural surroundings. I see Him in all His splendor in His creation and He often gives me small gifts from nature. I attended a men's conference in the Colorado Rockies surrounded by such beauty. After some teaching, we were to seek answers to some questions by asking God. As I sat atop a mountain in the sunshine with an eagle's cry piercing the air; I heard the Lord call me Joseph. This is, in fact, my middle name but He told me it was my new name and said that it fits me well as I have always been a dreamer. Since that day, when I quiet myself down to spend time with Him, He will sometimes start the conversation with my first name, but when He starts with Joseph I have learned that what He wants to say is very important and to be particularly attentive.

I was able to come into the Kingdom through my friend Jesus and have enjoyed many years with the inner habitation of Holy Spirit. Due to my broken relationship with my earthly father, I found it more difficult to connect with God as my Father. Through much inner healing of my emotional hurts, I have come to know my Heavenly Father well. Irene and I have experienced emotional healing and as a result, now operate in spiritual gifts which have enabled us to minister inner healing to many others. Increasingly, as I spend time and focus my attention on Him, I have also grown in hearing God through dreams and visions. Often they are very personal but I have been given visions for others, especially during prayer times and inner healing sessions. As we intentionally pray and give these sessions over to Holy Spirit, we ask the participants questions as He leads us. We often see others become activated in hearing and seeing God in various ways, as they go through the healing process.

As I continue to walk and grow in the different ways God speaks to me, my faith has increased to believe in and use these precious gifts from Holy Spirit. I belong to a growing community, a fellowship of believers, open to what our Triune God has to say to us as we walk out His Kingdom here on this earth. By opening our heart, mind, soul, and spirit to the depth of God's love for us we, in turn, are seeing others as He sees them. Jesus came into the world to demonstrate the Father's love for all mankind. We, in turn, are to love others as He does.

Rev. Virginia's Story
Hearing God through Words and Thoughts

Has anyone ever told you that you can hear God's voice? I would hear people talk about hearing God's voice, but no one ever told me how to hear or what God's voice actually sounds like.

I knew that sometimes I would hear a voice or have thoughts that were not my own - thoughts of good things or thoughts of evil; thoughts that were totally new that I didn't spend time thinking about, and thoughts that I didn't want to think. It reminded me of a little comic I once saw - of a person with a little devil sitting on one shoulder and a little angel sitting on the other shoulder. Both were whispering ideas into the person's ears. Have you ever had that happen? I knew in my heart that I wanted to think good thoughts. I didn't want to think evil thoughts, but I couldn't seem to stop the evil ones from entering my mind. When I really stopped to think about it I realized that I hadn't thought those bad thoughts up - they just seemed to pop in - and come to think about it - the good ones just popped in too!

One thing that I did realize though, that helped me know I was hearing God's voice, was that He would often use words I didn't even use. As a matter of fact, I often had to look them up in a dictionary to see if they fit the context of what I was hearing - and they always did! I was amazed and began to believe I was really hearing God's voice.

The other thing that I noticed was that when I would hear God speaking to me it was always much nicer than I would ever talk to myself! I wondered, "Does He talk to everyone this way?" The other thing I realized that help me know it was God speaking to me was that Satan wouldn't say things that were that loving and kind. I was beginning to believe that I was actually hearing God's voice.

For some reason, near the beginning, I became afraid that God might say something to me that I might not like, so I stopped actively listening for His voice. I didn't hear Him again for quite a while. One day when I least expected to hear God's voice He spoke to me saying, "You can trust Me with your life because I trusted you with My life." I knew right away that He was saying that even if I never accepted His sacrifice for myself - He still went to the cross for me. From that moment on I believed I was hearing Him and that I didn't need to be afraid of anything He would tell me. That was an amazing breakthrough for me!

A few years later a friend invited me to hear Mark Virkler teaching a seminar on Hearing God's Voice. Mark's teaching confirmed that I was actually hearing God's voice. He taught us about the way you can tell what thoughts your own and what thoughts are not your own. He told us that when we are thinking our own thoughts our mind is actually working, turning things over, adding things up, planning, or evaluating something. He also told us that the thoughts that just pop into our mind we can't take credit for because we didn't actually think them up. Those thoughts were either from God (Holy Spirit) or from Satan.

That is when I began to realize that sometimes Satan had been tempting me with evil thoughts, thoughts of shame, doubt, sin, fear, rage, jealousy, pride, lust, etc., but it was my choice whether to continue thinking about them or reject them. I also realized that God was giving me His thoughts that are always pure, good, loving, kind, hopeful, peaceful, creative, and encouraging.

Everything good comes from God and He wants us to follow His heart of love in every situation. God has an opinion about everything that is going on in our lives and knows the answer to every difficult situation we face. All we need to do is ask! And then listen! I have realized since that seminar that I can also hear God through seeing with the eyes of my heart. Hearing him through the still small voice inside was the first way I learned to hear Him and I would say that is my "first language", but I now hear Him often through dreams or visions, touch, and smell. I have yet to experience "taste" and I am looking forward to that day!

Knowing how to hear and know God's voice has set me on a different course in my Christian life! It has given me a passion to help others learn to hear His voice too. It has opened ministry opportunities I never dreamed of. I now actively listen for God's voice every day and He so lovingly guides me, corrects me, and teaches me things I never knew before. It is so wonderful to know Jesus in this intimate way. I can talk to Him and He answers me in ways I often don't even expect! He is amazing and He wants to be our very best friend - one we commune with every day - in many ways! I pray you will learn to hear His voice and come into greater intimacy with our loving Saviour.

Rev. Yvonne's Experience
Hearing God through Dreams

Throughout my life, God has been speaking to me through dreams. When I was very young I had vivid dreams, many of which were quite frightening. I remember lots of times climbing into my parents' bed crying and afraid. My dreams were so real. I had multi-sensory experiences involving taste, touch, and smell. I would fall from great heights (landing with a soft kind of bounce). I was chased by evil people.

Of course, I had many fun dreams too but the nightmares were disturbing and often repetitive. The odd thing was I was drawn to supernatural experiences even though I was afraid of them. I would watch frightening movies as a teenager and was fascinated with the foretelling of the future. This fascination led to some quite overt and frightening supernatural experiences. The God-given dream and vision capacity had been clouded by fear of evil and involvement in ungodly encounters. I had such frightening encounters that eventually I told God (even though I didn't believe in Him at the time) I did not want to see anything supernatural or weird. Funny thing about telling God things when you are not even sure He is there....He tends to act, which is what happened. My dream and visionary capacity shut down. I was oblivious to the fact that God wants to reveal Himself to us and He listens to our prayers, so I didn't really notice He had stopped the nasty dreams. I continued on in my unbelieving lifestyle, fulfilling some of my own nightmares that were given to warn me and keep me from harm.

God is so kind and showed me such mercy that many years later He won my heart and I became a Christian. For the first 20 years, I lived the Christian life in a logical, methodical, and rule-abiding way! Not very well, but I did try. As you can imagine, living by rules, going to Church out of duty and trying to be a good person was quite a dry, religious approach to spiritual life. In much the same spirit that I had told God to stop the weird stuff in my life, I now told Him I wanted Him to be real. I wanted to experience Him - to know He is with me. I'm sure He chuckled! As I said, God is merciful and after some very needed repentance on my part for participating in occult practices, Jesus opened the door to the deeper life in the experience of His presence.

I needed to renounce more than just my involvement in ungodly things. The vows I had made had shut down the ability to dream and see in the spirit. God restored my dream life very suddenly (after a pastor prayed for me), then He slowly taught me to interpret the dreams. Later I also received the spiritual gift of dream interpretation. The visionary capacity slowly built as God taught me it was good to look for what He wanted me to see and taught me to fix my eyes on Jesus. I was apprehensive about waking visions because of demonic experiences which had frightened me as a teenager as well as some of the teachings I had believed which taught the supernatural gifts no longer operate. Again, I needed to renounce those beliefs and agree with God's word that I can look to see visions and fix my eyes on Jesus.

Since that time, God has used dreams in my life to warn me (as He did so many years earlier), to direct me, to educate me, give insight into relational issues and even give me creative ideas for business. Visions have become part of my everyday experience. As you will have read in this book, I practice the presence of Christ by seeing Him with me. I find my conversations with Him to be authenticated by His word in the Bible as well as the wisdom He gives me each day which works in the reality of my life.

Journaling conversation with God is one of the best devotional tools I have learned. As I journal daily, I find listening to God in this way has helped to bring clarity to the dreams and visions as well as other sensory experiences God gives me. Now I live from the experience of hearing, seeing, touching, tasting, and smelling as well as intuitively knowing what God is communicating. The capacities of my soul have been opened by His gracious Spirit so that I can live in the assurance of the presence of Jesus Christ each day. I read the Bible faithfully. Though it is not the only way I hear God it is my first go-to in testing all the revelation I receive. I love the written word and revelatory word of God. The Bible is the eternal word, still relevant and reliable. Along with the revelatory word, the Bible is my personal daily spiritual food. It fuels my spirit and aligns me with the presence of Jesus and the will of God.

I have learned to hear God's voice through words as well as pictures. I know that because God loves me. He wants to communicate with me so He has brought people and tools to help me hear Him. I am assured God will do the same for you, dear reader. He loves to communicate with us. Friendship is His deep desire. So open up and ask Him what He would like to say to you today. LISTEN UP! God is speaking words of affirmation. He desires to give you an abundant, joyful life flowing from the richness of knowing and loving Jesus Christ.

Thank You

It is my prayer that you have found this book helpful in your friendship with God. I would love to hear from you and it would be most helpful to have feedback. I encourage you to write a review to help other readers decide on this book.

Other Books

Divine Focus
Living in Union with God
Arranged as a trilogy, Divine Focus explores the subject of practicing the presence of Christ. It explains how humans may live in complete agreement with Father, Son and Holy Spirit. Communion with God moment by moment is modeled beautifully by our Jesus Christ, so each of the sections of this trilogy are named after His self-description.

Section 1: **"The Life"** examines Jesus Christ as our example and teacher on the subject of living in perfect focus.

Section 2: **"The Truth"** contains essays on truths which explain the path and process of being tuned to the presence of God.

Section 3: **"The Way"** details disciplines and practices which Christians through the ages have used to connect in intimate friendship with God.

The Restoration Work Book for Participants
A Guide to Restoring the Soul Through Inner-Healing
Developed from Biblical techniques, this approach to prayer counselling is used for Inner Healing of the personality or soul. It is a practical tool to enable every Christian to pray through areas of blockage and emotional pain. Once learned, this method can be used in subsequent areas of emotional pain and blockages to continue on the road of healing and restoration using the reproducible work sheets provided.

Chapter Headings:
- The Wounded Soul
- Seven Steps for Restoring the Soul
- Restoring Generational Lines
- Correcting Soul Ties

- Healing Painful Memories
- Renouncing Negative Words
- Renewing Truth and Purpose
- Cleansing from the Demonic
- Living by Holy Spirit's Power
- Aftercare
- Reproducible Resources

The Restoration Work Book Leaders Guide
A Leaders Guide to Restoring the Soul Through Inner-Healing
The Leader's Edition of the workbook is a manual for leaders of the restoration workshops. This book includes all material in Participant Guide as well as additional helps and methods to assist Inner-Healing leaders. This guide also contains prayers of repentance from Freemasonry.

The Language of Dreams and Visions
A Handbook for Interpretation and Symbolism
This handbook is a guide to understanding and interpreting dreams and visions. It contains an extensive and valuable dictionary of biblical and cultural symbols giving insight into God's way of communication. It includes a template dream journal for recording and interpreting dreams.

Chapters include:
- God Is Speaking
- Supernatural Encounters
- Defining Dream and Vision
- Restoring Dream and Visionary Capacities
- Soaking or Listening Prayer
- Dream and Vision Recording
- Interpretation
- Testing Revelation
- Dictionary of Symbols

- Biblical Reference Section for Dreams, Visions and Bible References for the Names of God

The Kingdom Within
Knowing God the Spirit and Learning to Flow In and Through Him

This book is for people looking for a primer on Holy Spirit (Holy Spirit 101). It will help you to learn about His nature, graces and gifts but even more importantly it is designed to draw you into a deeper friendship with God. It provides practical and easy ways for you to tune your heart to Him. Each chapter has suggested meditation questions which are designed to enable you to understand what God has for you.

Chapters include:
- Coming to Know the Holy Spirit – Progressing Toward Union With God
- Knowing Holy Spirit – His Name, Symbolic Descriptions, The Sevenfold Spirit
- Holy Spirit the Giver – Fruit of the Spirit, Gifts of the Spirit
- Positioned to Receive – Focus, Faith, Filled With the Spirit
- Revealer of Truth – How God Speaks, Our Spiritual Senses
- Spiritual Disciplines – Listening Prayer, Meditation, Fasting, Spiritual Retreat
- Testing Revelation
- Ministering through the Spirit – Praying Like Jesus, Releasing the Flow
- Teamwork – Prophetic Etiquette, Seeking God Together

Destiny Purpose and Calling
Understanding and Fulfilling Your Unique Place in God's Kingdom on Earth

A straight-forward, practical guide to bring you along in your journey of discovery as to who God has designed you to be, where you are in your journey of purpose in Him and what you next step along His path is. Every chapter includes action steps to intentionally move you into your purpose and calling so you may enjoy the journey into Kingdom destiny.

Chapters include:
- The Books of Destiny – My Legacy
- Created for Purpose
- Kingdom Calling
- Check the Baggage
- Personal Identity – Where Have I Come From? Who am I? Why am I Here?
- Gifts From God – Discerning My Spiritual Gifts
- Talents & Skills – Discerning My Abilities
- Additions or Distractions
- Tracking With God – Where am I @?
- Finding My Life in Him – Where am I Going?
- Getting to My Destination

About Yvonne

Once a native of Australia, Yvonne lives and works in Canada. She has been married to her husband Bob for more than 45 years. They have five grown children and eight adorable grandchildren. Yvonne has been a friend of God for over 40 years and is growing to love Him more each year. Under God's direction and anointing Yvonne produces:

- Customized prayer blankets
- Scripture meditation CD's
- Manuals & books on topics such as inner-healing, listening prayer, meditation, interpreting dreams and visions, knowing the Holy Spirit, and discerning destiny

Rev. Yvonne Prentice,

Pastor at His Presence Ministries

Credentialed with ECCiC

Yvonne brings encouragement and hope to many. She loves to introduce others to the practice of "soaking" or listening prayer, and Biblical meditation. She loves to foster times in God's presence helping others deepen their friendship with Jesus Christ. Regularly ministering at retreats and workshops, Yvonne's heart is to see God's people grow in intimacy with Jesus Christ by practicing His presence daily.

Contact

Email: hispresenceministries@gmail.com

Facebook: through her page *His Presence Ministries.*

Blog: pushingtheedges.blogspot.com

www.ingramcontent.com/pod-product-compliance
Lightning Source LLC
Chambersburg PA
CBHW060140050426
42448CB00010B/2226